Progressive Beginner

UKULELE

by
Peter Gelling

Visit our Website
www.learntoplaymusic.com

The Progressive Series of Music Instruction Books, CDs and DVDs

2

Published by
KOALA MUSIC^{TM}
PUBLICATIONS

Like us on Facebook
www.facebook.com/LearnToPlayMusic

View our YouTube Channel
www.youtube.com/learntoplaymusiccom

Follow us on Twitter
twitter.com/LTPMusic

Visit our Website
www.learntoplaymusic.com

PROGRESSIVE BEGINNER UKULELE
I.S.B.N. 978 982 9118 88 2
Order Code: 11888

Acknowledgments
Cover Photograph: Sarah Petrusma
Photographs: Sarah Petrusma

For more information on this series contact
LTP Publishing Pty Ltd
email: info@learntoplaymusic.com
or visit our website
www.learntoplaymusic.com

CONTENTS

INTRODUCTION

Progressive Beginner Ukulele provides an easy and enjoyable introduction to the world of Ukulele playing. No previous knowledge of music or the Ukulele is necessary.

Through the course of this book, you will learn how to play all the essential chords, using both open position and movable shapes, along with all the right hand strumming techniques and rhythms used in a wide variety of musical styles. All examples sound great and are fun to play. By the end of the book you will be able to play hundreds of songs and be well on your way to being an excellent Ukulele player.

To develop good timing habits right from the start, it is recommended that you use a **metronome or drum machine** with all the examples in the book until you can play them easily from memory. You should also learn to play the examples along with the recording.

The best and fastest way to learn is to use this book in conjunction with:

1. Buying sheet music of your favorite recording artists and learning to play their songs. By learning songs, you will begin to build a repertoire and always have something to play in jam sessions.
2. Practicing and playing with other musicians as often as possible.
3. Learning by listening to your favorite recordings. Start building a collection of albums of players you admire or wish to emulate. Try playing along with one of them for a short time each day. Most of the great Ukulele players have learned a lot of their music this way.

In the early stages it is helpful to have the guidance of an experienced teacher. This will also help you keep to a schedule and obtain weekly goals.

APPROACH TO PRACTICE

From the beginning you should set yourself a goal. Many people learn the Ukulele because of a desire to play like their favorite artist (e.g., Tiny Tim or Israel Kamakawiwo'ole), or to play a certain style of music (e.g., Hawaiian songs, Swing, etc.). Motivations such as these will help you to persevere through the more difficult sections of work. As you develop it will be important to adjust and update your goals.

It is important to have a correct approach to practice. You will benefit more from several short practices (e.g., 15-30 minutes per day) than one or two long sessions per week. This is especially so in the early stages, because of the basic nature of the material being studied. In a practice session you should divide your time evenly between the study of new material and the revision of past work. It is a common mistake for semi-advanced students to practice only the pieces they can already play well. Although this is more enjoyable, it is not a very satisfactory method of practice. You should also try to correct mistakes and experiment with new ideas.

USING THE ACCOMPANYING DVDS & CD

The accompanying DVDs and CD contain video and audio recordings of all of the examples in this book. An exercise number and a play button indicates a recorded example.

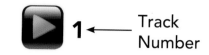

Track Number

The book instructs you how to play, while the recordings show you how each example should look and sound when performed correctly. Practice an example slowly at first, then try playing to a metronome set to a slow tempo so that you can play it evenly and without stopping. Gradually increase the tempo as you become more confident and then try playing along with the recording. You will hear a drum beat at the beginning of each example to lead you in and help you keep time.

Included with this book:

1 Audio CD containing exercises 1-99.

2 Video DVDs containing all exercises in the book. Each video demonstrates how to play the exercise and includes an animated score so you can read the music and play along. You can also choose between three audio options:

1. Full track - hear how the Ukulele should sound with a band
2. Solo part - listen to the Ukulele part by itself
3. Backing track - play along with the band!

These 'audio streams' (or language tracks) should be accessible from most DVD remotes.

1 DVD-ROM containing all exercises in the book. This disc contains video content for use with both Windows Media Player (included with most Windows PCs) and Apple iTunes/QuickTime Player (included with Apple computers and available for Windows at www.apple.com). The audio content is compatible with any MP3 compatible music player, including Windows Media Player and iTunes. The contents of this DVD-ROM should be compatible with most portable media players and gaming consoles (e.g., iPod, Xbox, Playstation etc.) Follow the instructions for your media player to import these files to your hard drive or transfer to your portable media player if required.

Tips
- Most DVD and portable media players have the ability to repeat tracks. You can make good use of this feature to practice the examples a number of times without stopping.
- The latest versions of Windows Media Player and QuickTime Player 7 (available for download from www.apple.com) have the ability to slow down music which is handy for practicing complicated pieces.

TUNING YOUR UKULELE

Before you commence each lesson or practice session you will need to tune your Ukulele. If your Ukulele is out of tune everything you play will sound incorrect even though you are holding the correct notes.

On the accompanying DVDs and DVD-ROM there are tuning notes which correspond to the **four strings of the Ukulele**. For a complete description of how to tune your Ukulele, see the methods shown at the end of the book.

HOW TO HOLD THE UKULELE

SITTING

1. Sit up straight on the front part of the chair as shown in the photo below.

2. The Ukulele should be close to your body in an upright position with the neck pointing slightly upwards.

3. Some players prefer to sit with their legs crossed. Experiment to find the sitting position which suits you best.

The main aim is to be comfortable and have easy access to the Ukulele fretboard. A music stand will also be helpful.

STANDING

Stand with your weight evenly balanced on both feet and tilt the neck slightly upwards.

USING THE PICK

The right hand is used to play the strings by plucking them with a pick. A pick is a piece of plastic shaped like a triangle.

Hold the pick lightly between your **thumb and first finger**, as shown in the following photo.

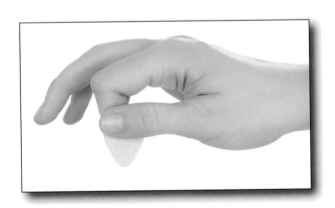

Use the tip of the pick to play the string.

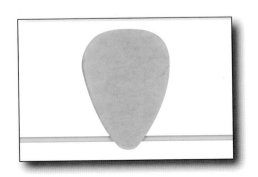

LEFT HAND TECHNIQUE

LEFT HAND POSITION

The left hand fingers are numbered as such:

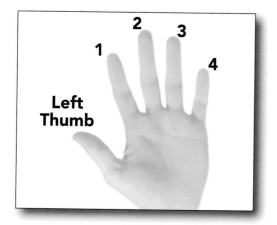

LEFT HAND PLACEMENT

Your fingers should be **ON THEIR TIPS** and placed just **BEHIND** the frets (not on top of them).

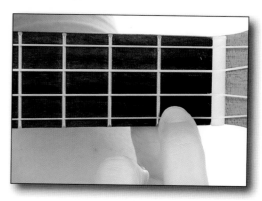

Be careful not to allow the thumb to hang too far over the top of the neck (Photo A), or to let it run parallel along the back of the neck (Photo B).

Photo A: INCORRECT

Photo B: INCORRECT

PARTS OF THE UKULELE

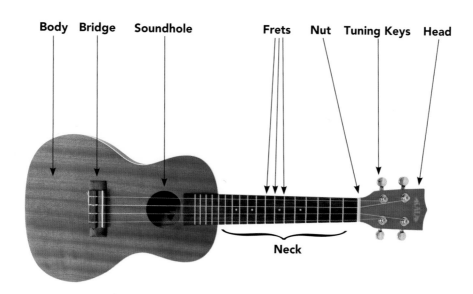

THE RUDIMENTS OF MUSIC

The musical alphabet consists of 7 letters: **A B C D E F G**

Music is written on a **staff**, which consists of 5 parallel lines between which there are 4 spaces.

MUSIC STAFF

The treble or 'G' clef is placed at the beginning of each staff line.

Treble or 'G' clef →

This clef indicates the position of the note G. It is an old fashioned method of writing the letter G, with the center of the clef being written on the second staff line.

G note

The other lines and spaces on the staff are named as such:

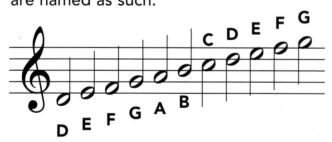

Extra notes can be added by the use of short lines, called **ledger lines**.

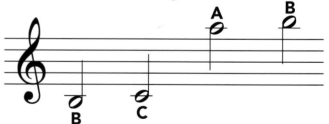

When a note is placed on the staff its head indicates its position, e.g.:

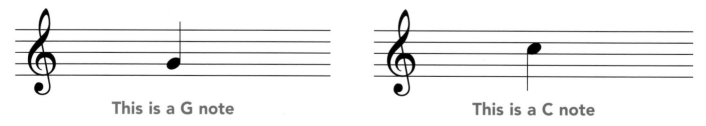

This is a G note

This is a C note

When the note head is below the middle staff line the stem points upward and when the head is above the middle line the stem points downward. A note placed on the middle line (**B**) can have its stem pointing either up or down.

Bar lines are drawn across the staff, which divides the music into sections called **bars** or **measures**. A **final bar line** signifies the end of the music.

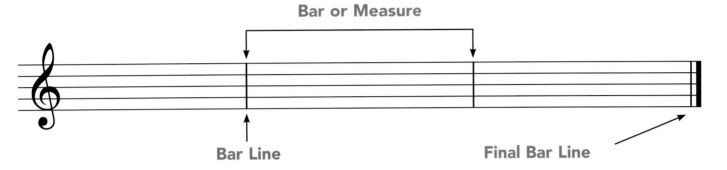

TIME SIGNATURES

At the beginning of each piece of music, after the treble clef, is the **time signature**.

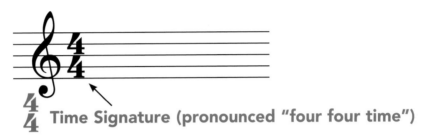

$\frac{4}{4}$ Time Signature (pronounced "four four time")

The time signature indicates the number of beats per bar (the top number) and the type of note receiving one beat (the bottom number). For example:

4 – this indicates 4 beats per bar.

4 – this indicates that each beat is worth a quarter note (crotchet).

Thus in $\frac{4}{4}$ time there must be the equivalent of 4 quarter note beats per bar, e.g.,

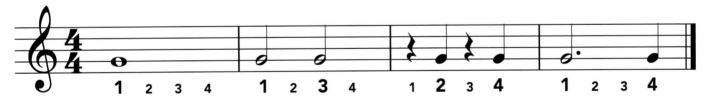

$\frac{4}{4}$ is the most common time signature and is sometimes represented by this symbol called **common time**.

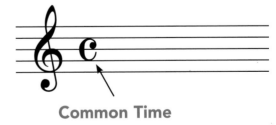

Common Time

The next most common time signature is **Three Four Time** written $\frac{3}{4}$.

$\frac{3}{4}$ indicates 3 quarter note beats per bar, as shown here.

NOTE VALUES

The table below sets out the most common notes used in music and their respective time values (i.e., length of time held). For each note value there is an equivalent rest, which indicates a period of silence.

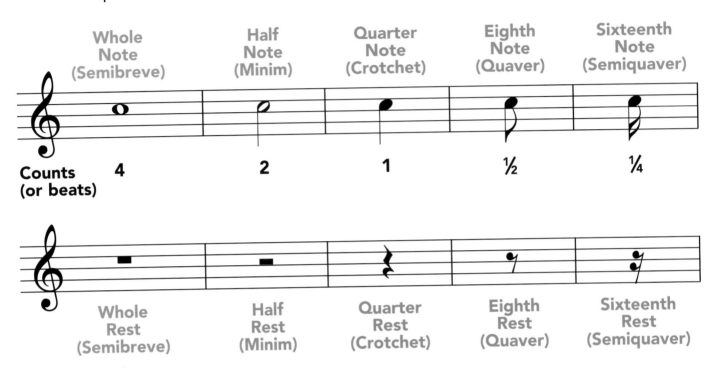

	Whole Note (Semibreve)	Half Note (Minim)	Quarter Note (Crotchet)	Eighth Note (Quaver)	Sixteenth Note (Semiquaver)
Counts (or beats)	4	2	1	½	¼
	Whole Rest (Semibreve)	Half Rest (Minim)	Quarter Rest (Crotchet)	Eighth Rest (Quaver)	Sixteenth Rest (Semiquaver)

If a **dot** is placed after a note, it increases the value of that note by half, e.g.:

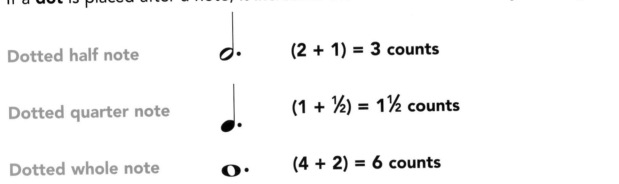

Dotted half note   (2 + 1) = 3 counts

Dotted quarter note   (1 + ½) = 1½ counts

Dotted whole note   (4 + 2) = 6 counts

The timing of basic note values, rhythms and rests can also be illustrated in the following table.

NOTES, RHYTHMS AND RESTS

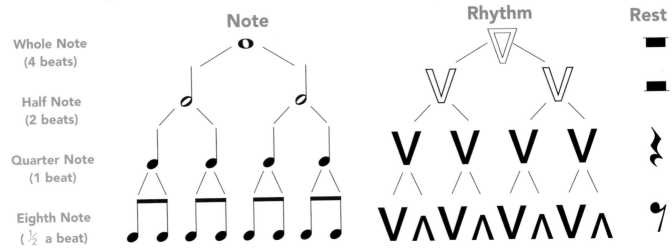

	Note	Rhythm	Rest
Whole Note (4 beats)			
Half Note (2 beats)			
Quarter Note (1 beat)			
Eighth Note (½ a beat)			

CHORD DIAGRAMS

Chords are learned with the help of a **chord diagram**. This will show you exactly where to place your left hand fingers in order to play a particular chord. A chord diagram is a grid of horizontal and vertical lines representing the strings and frets of the Ukulele as shown.

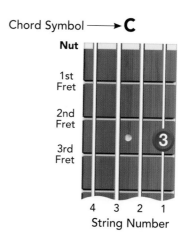

Chord Symbol ——▶ **C**

LEFT HAND FINGERING

① Index Finger ③ Ring Finger
② Middle Finger ④ Little Finger

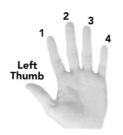

The **dots** show you where to place your left hand fingers. The **number** tells you which finger to place on the string just before the fret. If there is no dot on a string, you play it as an open (not fretted) string.

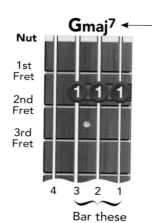

Chord symbol for G major seventh chord.

A small **bar** connecting two or more dots indicates that they are held down by the same finger. This is called **barring.**

RHYTHM SYMBOLS

Count 1 2

This is a **half note strum**. It lasts for **two** beats. There are **two** half note strums in one bar of 4/4 time.

Count 1 +

This is a pair of **eighth note strums**. Each strum lasts for **half a beat**. There are **eight** eighth note strums in one bar of 4/4 time. Play the larger downward strum louder.

Count 1 + a

This is a group of three **eighth note triplet strums**. Each strum in the group lasts for **one third** of a beat. There are **twelve** eighth note triplet strums in one bar of 4/4 time. Play the larger downward strum louder.

Count 1

This is a **quarter note strum**. It lasts for **one** beat. There are **four** quarter note strums in one bar of 4/4 time.

Count 1 e + a

This is a group of **sixteenth note strums**. Each strum lasts for **one quarter** of a beat. There are **sixteen** sixteenth note strums in one bar of 4/4 time. Play the larger downward strum louder.

A broken strum symbol indicates that the strings are not to be strummed.

THE C MAJOR CHORD

A **chord** is a group of three or more notes played together. Chords are used to accompany a singer, or an instrumentalist who is playing the melody of a song. The first chord you will learn is the **C major chord**, usually just called the **C chord**. The **C major** chord is indicated by the letter **C**. This is called the **chord symbol**.

C

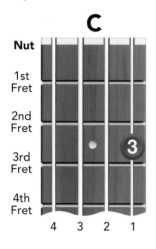

Nut
1st Fret
2nd Fret
3rd Fret
4th Fret

4 3 2 1

C Major Chord

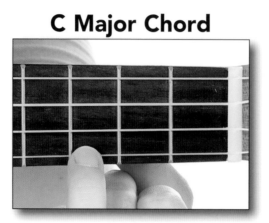

Chord Symbol

C

To play the **C** chord, place the **third** finger of your left hand just behind the **third** fret of the **first** string. The other three strings are played as open strings.

STRUMMING

Play **all four** strings at the same time with your index finger, thumb or pick, using a **downward** motion. This is called a **strum.** Hold the pick lightly and strum from the wrist. Keep your wrist relaxed. If any notes buzz or sound deadened, you may have to press harder with the left hand fingers and make sure that your fingers are just behind the fret.

Strumming with the first finger

Strumming with the thumb

Strumming with the fingers

Strumming with the pick

QUARTER NOTE STRUM

V This is the symbol for a downward **quarter note strum**. It lasts for **one beat**. There are **four** quarter note strums in one bar of $\frac{4}{4}$ time.

Count: **1**

WHOLE NOTE STRUM

This is a **whole note strum**. It lasts for **four beats**. There is **one** whole note strum in one bar of $\frac{4}{4}$ time.

Count: **1** 2 3 4

In the following example there are five bars of the **C major** chord played in $\frac{4}{4}$ time. The chord symbol is written above the staff and is placed at the beginning of each bar. Play the chord with four quarter note strums in each bar. To make the example sound complete, always end with a whole note strum $\mathbb{V}$ of the first chord, as shown at the end of this example.

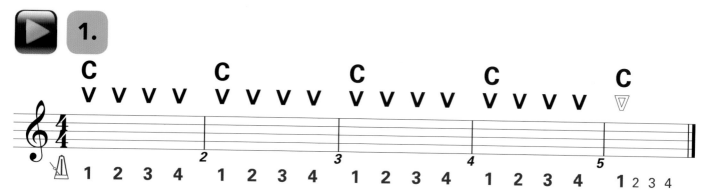

THE SEVENTH CHORD

Another type of common chord is the **dominant seventh** chord. It is usually referred to as the **seventh** chord. The chord symbol for the seventh chord is the number **7** written after the alphabetical letter. The symbol for the **G seventh** chord is **G7**.

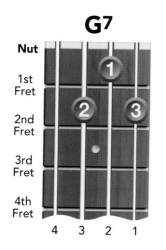

G Seventh Chord

Chord Symbol

G⁷

To play the **G7** chord, place the **first, second** and **third** fingers of your left hand as shown in the diagram. Strum all **four** strings.

THE HALF NOTE STRUM

Count: 1 2

This is a **half note strum**.
It lasts for **two** beats.
There are **two** half note strums in one bar of $\frac{4}{4}$ time.

The example below contains five bars of the **G7** chord. Play two half note strums in each bar. The **bold** numbers tell you to strum the chord, the **smaller** numbers indicate to hold it until the next strum.

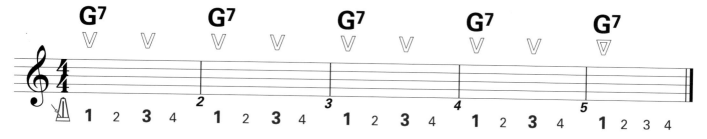

CHORD PROGRESSIONS

The following example is called a **chord progression**, meaning **a series of chord changes** (in this case between **C** and **G7**). Chord progressions are common in all styles of music, and the more you know, the more songs you will be able to play. The two dots at the end of bar 4 are a repeat sign, telling you to play again from the start.

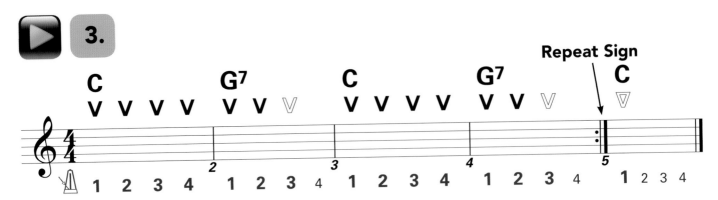

SLIDE FINGER

When changing from **C** to **G7**, do not lift your third finger off the first string, but slide it down to the second fret. Only touch the string very lightly as you slide along it. The use of the slide finger will make changing between C and G7 chords easier.

RHYTHM PATTERNS

Instead of writing the strumming above each bar of music, it is easier to write it as a **rhythm pattern**. This indicates which strumming pattern to use in each bar throughout the song. The rhythm pattern above the following example shows four strums per bar, with each strum having the value of a quarter note. At the end of the song, play a final C chord and let it ring.

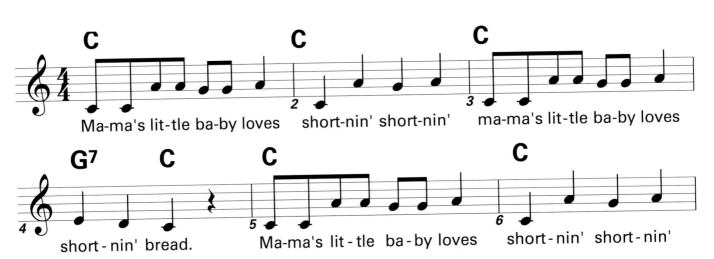

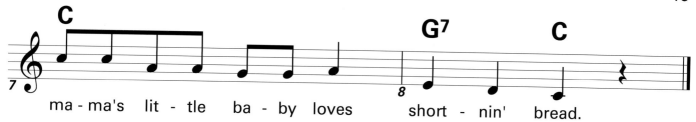

ma - ma's lit - tle ba - by loves short - nin' bread.

 5. Mary Ann

This traditional Caribbean song also uses the chords **C** and **G7** and sounds great on the Ukulele. Remember to use the slide finger technique when changing chords.

Rhythm Pattern

V V V V
1 2 3 4

All day all night Ma - ry Ann,_____

_____ Down by the sea - side

sif - ting sand,_____ All the lit - tle

chil - dren love Ma - ry Ann_____

Down by the sea - side sif - ting sand_____

LESSON TWO

F

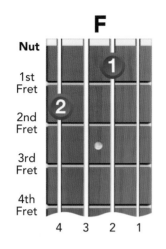

Nut
1st Fret
2nd Fret
3rd Fret
4th Fret

4 3 2 1

F Major Chord

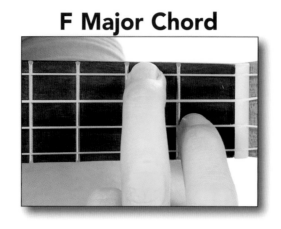

Chord Symbol

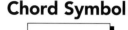

| F |

To play the **F** chord, use the **first** and **second** fingers of your left hand as shown in the diagram. Strum **all four** strings.

PIVOT FINGER

When changing between the **F** and **G7** chords, do not move your first finger as it is common to both chords. The first finger acts as a **pivot** around which the other fingers move. This will make the chord changes easier.

▶ **6.**

Rhythm Pattern

V   V
1 2 **3** 4

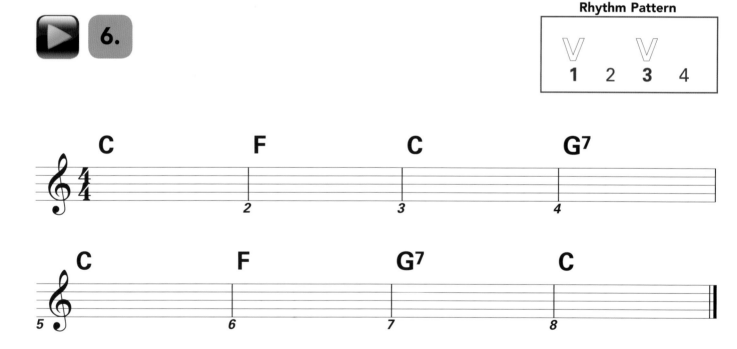

C   F   C   G⁷

3/4 4/4

2   3   4

C   F   G⁷   C

5   6   7   8

OPEN CHORD SHAPES

All the chord shapes you are learning here are examples of **open chords**, which means they contain open strings (i.e., no finger is placed on the fret). Later in the book, you will learn other chord types (e.g., bar chords) which do not contain open strings.

THE LEAD-IN

Sometimes a song does not begin on the first beat of the bar. Any notes which come before the first full bar are called **lead-in notes** (or **pick-up notes**). When lead-in notes are used, the last bar is also incomplete. The notes in the lead-in and the notes in the last bar add up to one full bar. When you are playing chords, do not strum until the first full bar after the lead-in notes.

  7. When The Saints Go Marchin' In

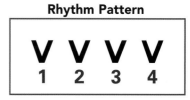

Practice each of the chord changes and then play the whole song. When changing between the **F** and **G7** chords, use your **first** finger as a **pivot**. When changing between **G7** and **C**, **slide** your **third** finger along the **first** string.

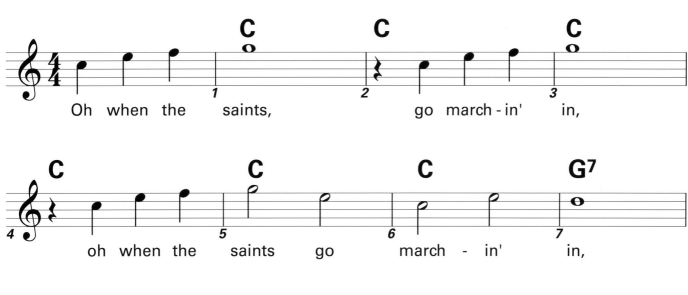

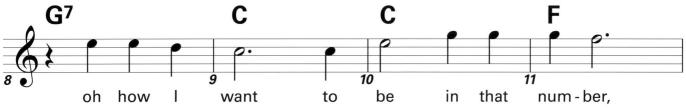

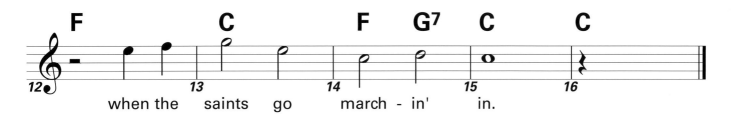

12 BAR BLUES

The **12 Bar Blues** is a pattern of chords which repeat every 12 bars. There are hundreds of songs based on this chord progression, i.e., they contain basically the same chords in the same order. The 12 Bar Blues pattern is commonly used in Rock music and is the basis of Blues music.

Some well-known songs which use this 12 bar chord pattern are:

Original Batman TV Theme
Rock Around the Clock - Bill Haley
Johnny B Goode - Chuck Berry
Blue Suede Shoes - Elvis Presley
In the Mood - Glenn Miller
Surfin' USA - The Beach Boys

In the Summertime - Mungo Jerry
Long Tall Glasses - Leo Sayer
Killing Floor - Jimi Hendrix
Stuck in the Middle With You - Stealer's Wheel
Give Me One Reason - Tracy Chapman
Why Didn't You Call Me? - Macy Gray

The following 12 Bar Blues is in the **key of C major**. When a song is said to be in the key of **C major**, it means that the most important chord (and usually the first chord) is the **C** chord.

This pattern of chords will probably sound familiar to you. Instead of writing a chord symbol above each bar of music, it is common to only write a chord symbol when the chord changes. For example, the first four bars of this Blues are all **C** chords, played according to the rhythm pattern. To help keep time, **accent** (play louder) the first strum of every bar. End this 12 Bar Blues by strumming a **C** chord.

Rhythm Pattern

V	V	V	V
1	2	3	4

8. 12 Bar Blues in C

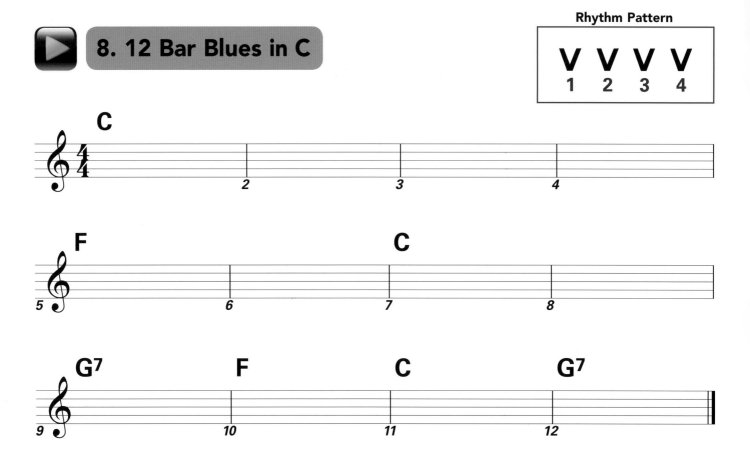

LESSON THREE

EIGHTH NOTE RHYTHMS

All the rhythm patterns you have played so far use a downward strum (V), on the first, second, third and fourth beat. To make rhythm patterns more interesting, **up strums** can also be used. An **eighth note rhythm** uses a combination of a down and an up strum within one beat. The downstrum "on the beat" is played louder than the upstrum which is "off the beat".

An **up strum** is indicated by a ∧, and is played on the "**and**" section of the count. To play an upstrum, start the strum at the **first** string and strum all four strings.

V ∧

Count: 1   +
Say: one   and

There are **two** eighth note strums per beat.
There are **eight** eighth note strums in one bar of music in ¼ time.
The downstrum "on the beat" is played louder than the upstrum which is "off the beat" (the '+' section of the count).

EIGHTH NOTE RHYTHM PATTERNS

Here are some **eighth note rhythm patterns** in ¼ time. Practice them while holding a **C** chord and then apply these patterns to the chord progressions in Lessons One and Two. Any of these patterns can be used on any chord progression in ¼ time.

9.   Pattern 1

V V∧V V
1 2 + 3 4

10.   Pattern 2

V V V∧V
1 2 3 + 4

11.   Pattern 3

V V∧V∧V∧
1 2 + 3 + 4 +

12.   Pattern 4

V V∧V∧V
1 2 + 3 + 4

13.   Pattern 5

V∧V∧V∧V∧
1 + 2 + 3 + 4 +

14.   Pattern 6

V∧V∧V V∧
1 + 2 + 3   4 +

15.   Pattern 7

V∧V V V
1 + 2 3 4

16.   Pattern 8

V∧V∧V V
1 + 2 + 3 4

17.   Pattern 9

V∧V∧V∧V
1 + 2 + 3 + 4

18.   Pattern 10

V V V V∧
1 2 3 4 +

19.   Pattern 11

V∧V V∧V
1 + 2 3 + 4

20.   Pattern 12

V V∧V V∧
1 2 + 3 4 +

G

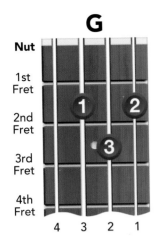

Nut
1st Fret
2nd Fret
3rd Fret
4th Fret

4 3 2 1

G Major Chord

Chord Symbol

G

To play the **G** chord, place the **first, second** and **third** fingers of your left hand as shown in the diagram. Strum all **four** strings.

The following chord progression contains a G chord and uses eighth note **rhythm pattern 1**.

21.

Rhythm Pattern

V V ∧V V
1 2 + 3 4

C   F   G   C

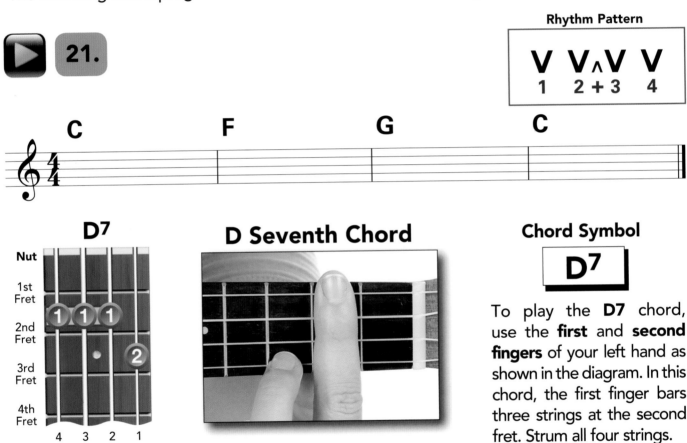

D⁷

Nut
1st Fret
2nd Fret
3rd Fret
4th Fret

4 3 2 1

D Seventh Chord

Chord Symbol

D⁷

To play the **D7** chord, use the **first** and **second fingers** of your left hand as shown in the diagram. In this chord, the first finger bars three strings at the second fret. Strum all four strings.

Practice new chord changes using a basic rhythm pattern first. Once you are confident with the progression, use the eighth note rhythm pattern. You can apply any rhythm pattern to a chord progression. This one uses eighth note **rhythm pattern 2**.

22.

Rhythm Pattern

V V V∧V
1 2 3 + 4

G   C   D⁷   G

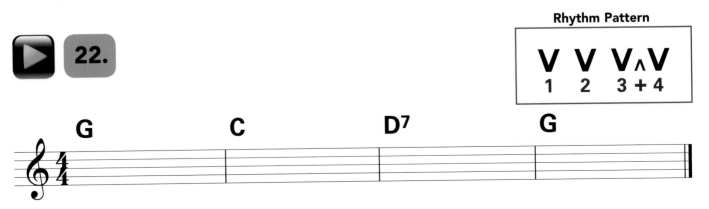

23. Oh Susannah

Stephen Foster

This song uses eighth note **rhythm pattern 4.** On the recording there are three drum beats to introduce this song.

LESSON FOUR

D
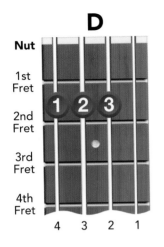

Nut
1st Fret
2nd Fret
3rd Fret
4th Fret

4 3 2 1

D Major Chord

Chord Symbol

To play the **D** chord, place the **first, second** and **third** fingers of your **left** hand as shown in the diagram, and strum all **four** strings.

When learning new chords, try to memorize the shape and visualize it before placing your fingers on the fretboard. When changing chords, hold down the current chord but visualize the next chord you are about to change to. This will solidify all the chords in your memory and will make chord changes easier.

 24.

Rhythm Pattern

V V V
1 2 3 4

G C D G

 25.

In this chord progression there are two chords in each bar. Each chord lasts for **two** beats. The rhythm pattern has two half note strums, so each chord is strummed once.

Rhythm Pattern

V V
1 2 3 4

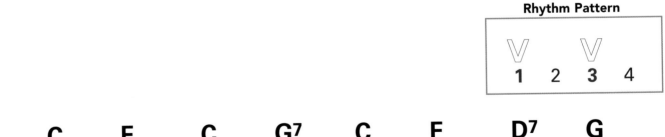

C F C G⁷ C F D⁷ G

C F C G⁷ C D G⁷ C

26. Sloop John B

The following song **Sloop John B** is a well-known American folk song. This song is in $\frac{4}{4}$ time and is in the key of **G major**. Play the chords using the rhythm pattern shown here.

LESSON FIVE

A
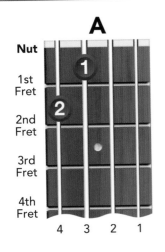

Nut
1st Fret
2nd Fret
3rd Fret
4th Fret

4 3 2 1

27.

The next exercise uses the A Major chord.

A Major Chord
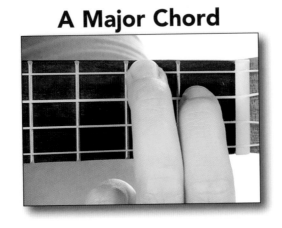

Chord Symbol

A

To play the **A** chord, place the **first** and **second** fingers of your left hand as shown in the diagram. Strum all **four** strings.

Rhythm Pattern

V V V
1 2 3 4

C	A	D⁷	G⁷

$\clubsuit$ $\frac{4}{4}$

A⁷
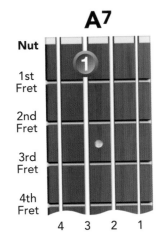

Nut
1st Fret
2nd Fret
3rd Fret
4th Fret

4 3 2 1

28.

This progression contains an **A7** chord and uses eighth note rhythm pattern **8**. When changing between **G7** and **C** use your **third** finger as a **slide** finger.

A Seventh Chord
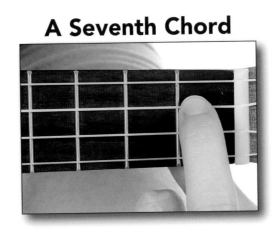

Chord Symbol

A⁷

To play the **A7** chord, use the **first** finger of your left hand as shown in the diagram, and strum all **four** strings. The **A7** chord shape is just an **A** chord shape with the **second** finger lifted off.

Rhythm Pattern

V∧V∧V V
1 + 2 + 3 4

C	A⁷	D⁷	G⁷

$\clubsuit$ $\frac{4}{4}$

This classic song by Hank Williams is in the key of D and uses the chords **D**, **A** and **A7**. Make sure you are comfortable with all the chord changes and then try them with the strumming pattern. Once you can play the song slowly, gradually increase the tempo until you can play it along with the recording.

E Seventh Chord

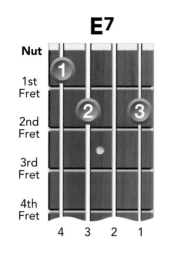

E7

Nut
1st Fret
2nd Fret
3rd Fret
4th Fret

4 3 2 1

Chord Symbol

To play the **E7** chord, use the **first**, **second** and **third** fingers of your left hand as shown in the diagram, and strum all **four** strings.

 30.

The following chord progression contains an **E7** chord and uses eighth note **rhythm pattern 1**.

When changing between **D** and **E7** use your **first** finger as a **slide** finger.

Rhythm Pattern

V V∧V V
1 2 + 3 4

D | E7 | G | A

31. Blues in A

Rhythm Pattern

V V∧V∧V
1 2 + 3 + 4

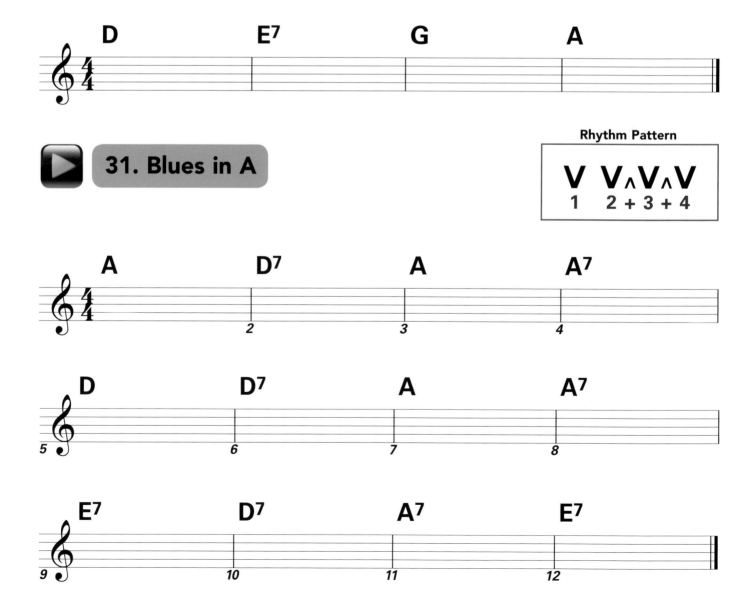

A | D7 | A | A7
2 | 3 | 4

D | D7 | A | A7
5 | 6 | 7 | 8

E7 | D7 | A7 | E7
9 | 10 | 11 | 12

B

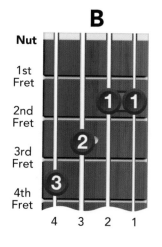

B Major Chord

Chord Symbol

B

To play the **B** chord, use the **first**, **second** and **third** fingers of your left hand as shown in the diagram, and strum all **four** strings.

32. Red Hot Peppers

This chord progression uses the B chord shown above. The progression is similar to the Blues song "They're Red Hot" by Robert Johnson and also recorded by the Red Hot Chili Peppers. Once you can play this progression, you will also be able to play many similar songs from the 1920s and 30s.

Rhythm Pattern

V V V V
1 2 3 4

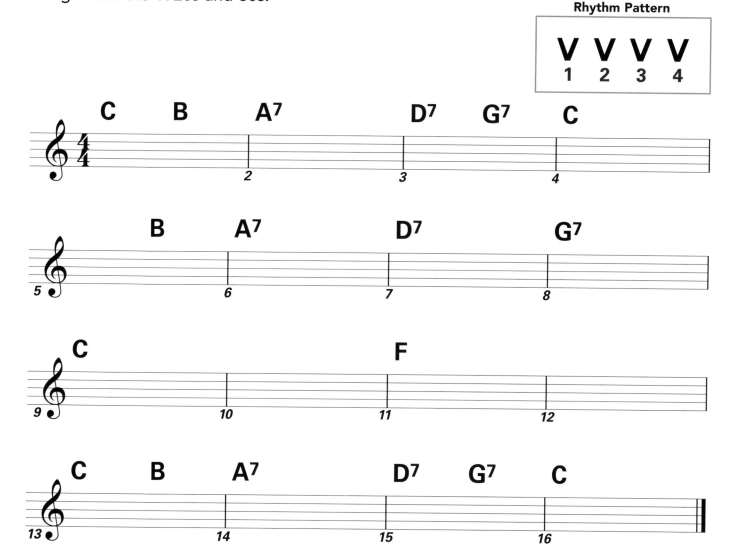

LESSON SEVEN

MINOR CHORDS

There are three main types of chords: **Major**, **Seventh**, and **Minor**. The chord symbol for the **minor** chord is a small 'm' placed after the letter name. Here are some commonly used minor chord shapes.

Dm

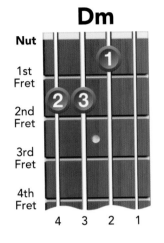

D Minor Chord

Chord Symbol

Dm

To play the **Dm** chord, use the **first**, **second** and **third** fingers of your left hand as shown in the diagram. Strum all **four** strings.

 33.

Rhythm Pattern

V V∧V∧V
1 2 + 3 + 4

Practice all the individual chord changes and then play the full progression. Make sure all the chords are clear and even.

| C | A⁷ | Dm | G⁷ |

Am

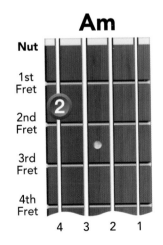

A Minor Chord

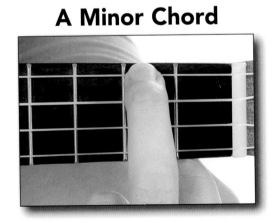

Chord Symbol

Am

To play the **Am** chord, use the **second** finger of your left hand as shown in the diagram. Strum all **four** strings.

 34.

Rhythm Pattern

V∧V∧V∧V
1 + 2 + 3 + 4

| Am | Dm | Am | E⁷ |

 ## 35. God Rest Ye Merry Gentlemen

This traditional Christmas song uses the chords **Am** and **Dm** along with **E7**, **C** and **F**. Make sure you are comfortable with all the chord changes and then play the song using the rhythm pattern shown.

Rhythm Pattern

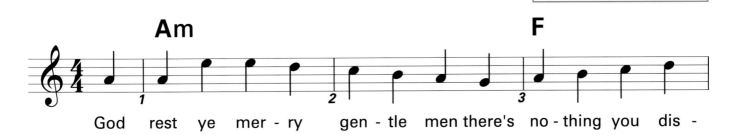

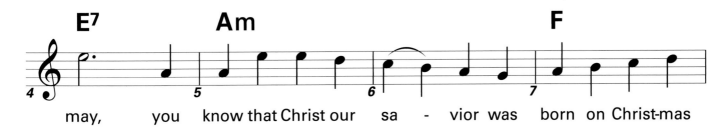

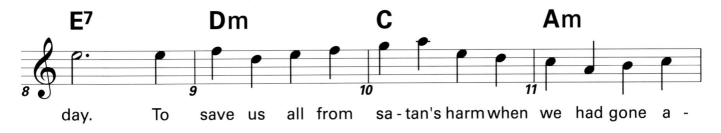

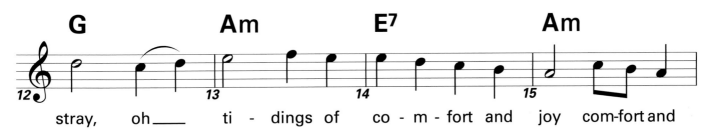

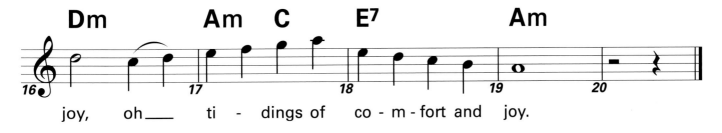

LESSON EIGHT

THE THREE FOUR TIME SIGNATURE

$\frac{3}{4}$ This is the **three four time signature**. It indicates that there are **three** beats in each bar. Three four time is also known as waltz time. There are three quarter notes in one bar of $\frac{3}{4}$ time.

The following chord progression is in $\frac{3}{4}$ time. To help keep time, **accent** (play louder) the first strum in each bar. Use your **first** finger as a **pivot** when changing between **Dm** and **G7**.

  36.

Rhythm Pattern

```
       C              Am             Dm            G7
```
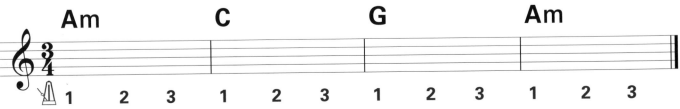

C   Am   Dm   G⁷

1 2 3   1 2 3   1 2 3   1 2 3

$\frac{3}{4}$ TIME RHYTHM PATTERNS

Practice the following $\frac{3}{4}$ **time rhythm patterns** holding a **C** chord shape. Apply any of these patterns to the above chord progression.

 **37.**

V   V ∧ V
1   2 + 3

38.

V ∧ V   V
1 + 2   3

 39.

V   V   V ∧
1   2   3 +

 40.

V ∧ V ∧ V
1 + 2 + 3

 41.

V   V ∧ V ∧
1   2 + 3 +

42.

V ∧ V ∧ V ∧
1 + 2 + 3 +

 Rhythm Pattern

V   V ∧ V
1   2 + 3

 43.

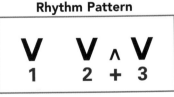

Am   C   G   Am

1 2 3   1 2 3   1 2 3   1 2 3

44. Scarborough Fair

Scarborough Fair contains the abbreviation **rit**, in bar 17, which stands for **ritardando**, meaning to **gradually slow down**.

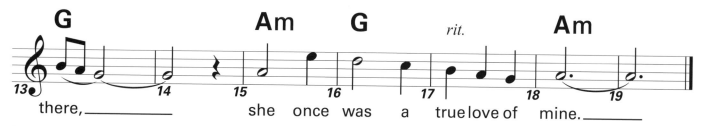

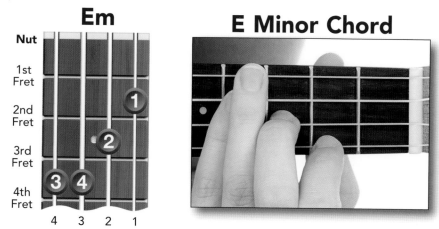

E Minor Chord

Chord Symbol

To play the **Em** chord, use **all four** fingers of your left hand as shown in the diagram. Strum all **four** strings.

The following chord progression is in ¾ time and uses three minor chords. Use your **first** finger as a **pivot** when changing between **Dm** and **G7**. Notice the use of a two bar rhythm pattern for this example.

Suggested Rhythm Pattern

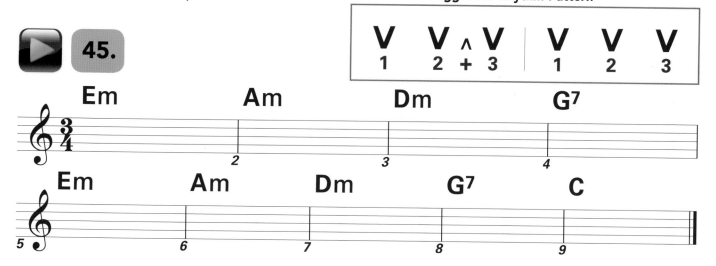

46. Morning Has Broken

Morning Has Broken is a well-known folk song in ¾ time.

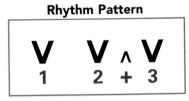

47. Molly Malone

This traditional Irish song is also in ¾ time.

Rhythm Pattern

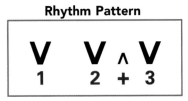

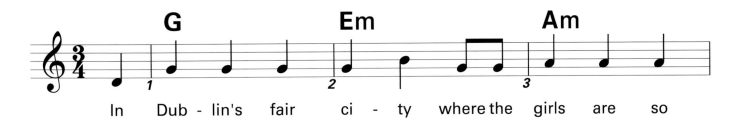

In Dub - lin's fair ci - ty where the girls are so

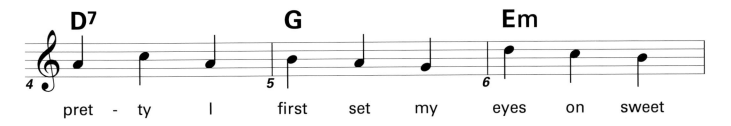

pret - ty I first set my eyes on sweet

Mol - ly Ma - lone, She wheeled a wheel -

bar - row through streets broad and nar - row crying

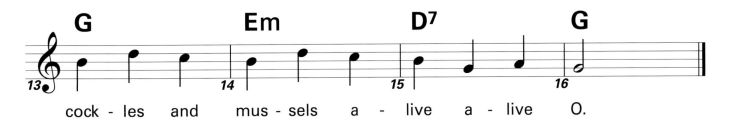

cock - les and mus - sels a - live a - live O.

LESSON NINE

THE SIX EIGHT TIME SIGNATURE

6/8 This is the **six eight** time signature.
There are six eighth notes in one bar of 6/8 time.
The six eighth notes are divided into two groups of three.

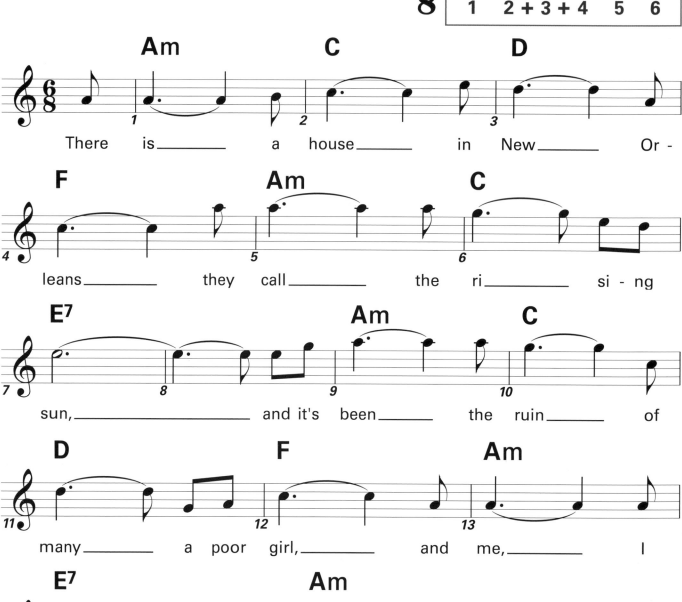

Count: **1 2 3 4 5 6** or **1** 2 3 **4** 5 6

In 6/8 time there are **two** pulses within each bar, with each beat being a **dotted quarter note**. (This is different to 4/4 and 3/4 time where each beat is a quarter note). **Accent** (play louder) the 1 and 4 count to help establish the two pulses per bar.

48. House of The Rising Sun

Suggested Rhythm Pattern

Am There is ___ a house ___ in New ___ Or-

C **D**

F leans ___ they call ___ the ri ___ si - ng

Am **C**

E⁷ sun, ___ and it's been ___ the ruin ___ of

Am **C**

D many ___ a poor girl, ___ and me, ___ I

F **Am**

E⁷ know ___ I'-m one.

Am

49. Daisy Bell (A Bicycle Built for Two)

TURNAROUND PROGRESSIONS

In an earlier lesson you were introduced to the 12 Bar Blues chord progression. Another common chord progression is called the **turnaround**. Like the 12 Bar Blues, it is the basis of many songs, and will probably sound familiar. Unlike the 12 Bar Blues, where the progression occurs over a fixed number of bars, the turnaround progression may vary in length as in the examples below, however the chord sequence remains the same. Some of the biggest hits of all time are based on the turnaround progression. Every year since the beginning of Rock music there have been hit songs based on turnaround progressions.

Stand by Me - John Lennon
I Will Always Love You - Whitney Houston
Return to Sender - Elvis Presley
All I Have to do is Dream - Everly Brothers
Always Look on the Bright Side of Life - Monty Python

The Young Ones - The Young Ones
Hungry Heart - Bruce Springsteen
Everlasting Love - U2
Last Kiss - Pearl Jam

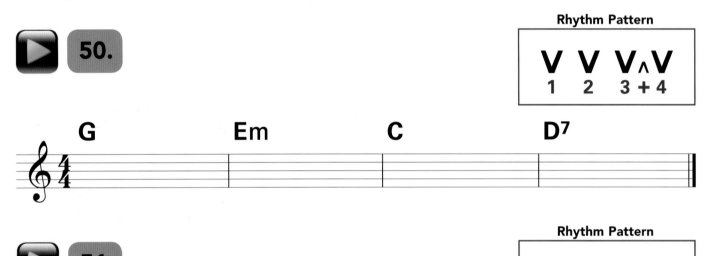

In this turnaround there are two chords in each bar.

Notice the similarity in sound in the turnaround progressions above. They are the **same** progression but in two different keys.

STRUMMING WITH THE THUMB

Up to this point, you have been strumming with a pick or the index finger. Another common Ukulele technique is to play down strums with the index finger and up strums with the thumb. Watch the video of the following example to see this technique in action.

In this turnaround there are two bars of each chord.

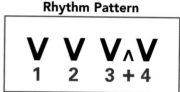

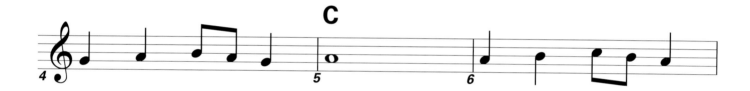

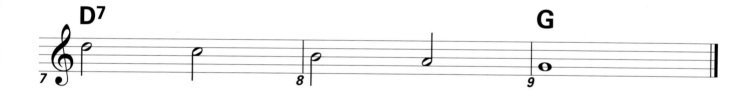

Here is a common variation on a turnaround in C with two chords per bar.

LESSON ELEVEN

SILENT STRUMS AND CONTINUOUS RHYTHMS

The basic $\frac{4}{4}$ rhythm pattern learned in **Lesson 1** consisted of four down strums, i.e.:

V V V V
1 2 3 4

Watch your right hand as you play this pattern again. You will notice that your hand actually moves **up and down in a continuous motion**, but it only makes contact with the strings on the **down** strum (V). The silent upward motion can be represented by a broken upward strum (Ʌ) indicating a silent upward strum.

So the basic rhythm **could** be written as: ⟶

VɅVɅVɅVɅ
1 + 2 + 3 + 4 +

This rhythm pattern and the one above sound exactly the same.

When you play eighth note rhythms (see Lesson 3) you will see that your right hand also moves up and down in a continuous motion sometimes making contact with the string and sometimes not. Some very useful and interesting rhythm patterns can result by incorporating eighth note rhythms with **silent down strums**.

SILENT STRUM SYMBOLS

When an **upward** strum is made without contacting the strings it can be represented by: Ʌ

When a **downward** strum is made without contacting the strings it can be represented by:

 54.

Try the following rhythm holding a **C** chord.

Rhythm Pattern

V VɅV̌ɅV
1 2 + 3 + 4

This rhythm is the same as **eighth note rhythm pattern 4** in Lesson Three, except that the down strum on the third beat does not make contact with the strings. Practice this rhythm until you perfect it. You can apply it to any chord progression you like. This is a very important rhythm and will be the basis of many other rhythms.

Apply this rhythm pattern to the following chord progression. Use **pivot** and **slide** fingers where possible to make the chord changes easier.

Rhythm Pattern

▶ **55.**

V VɅV̌ɅV
1 2 + 3 + 4

C   Am   Dm   G⁷

$\frac{4}{4}$

Try a variation of this rhythm pattern on the following turnaround progression in the key of **G**.

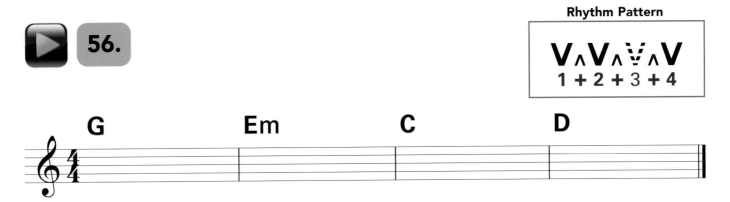

56.

Rhythm Pattern

V∧V∧V∧V
1 + 2 + 3 + 4

G   Em   C   D

This rhythm variation has a silent **down** strum on the 2nd and 3rd beat. Apply it to the following progression.

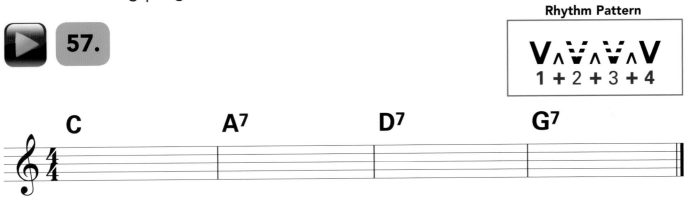

57.

Rhythm Pattern

V∧V∧V∧V
1 + 2 + 3 + 4

C   A⁷   D⁷   G⁷

RHYTHM VARIATIONS

Try the following rhythm variations and make up your own. Apply these rhythms to any chord progression you like. The **C chord** is used on the recording. All these variations are in $\frac{4}{4}$ time, but the same principle can be applied to $\frac{3}{4}$ time. Also note that in all these rhythms your **right** hand moves up and down in a **continuous motion**. These rhythm patterns can sound "off the beat". This is called **syncopation**.

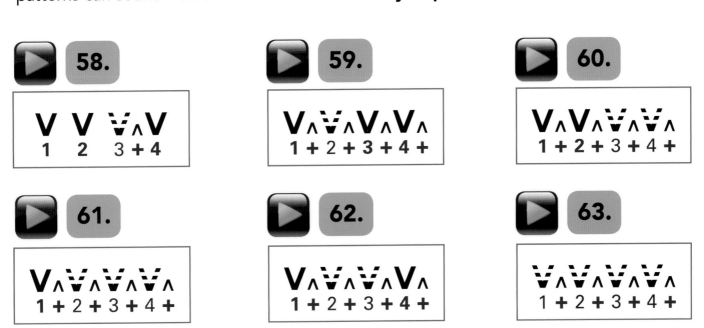

58.

V V V∧V
1 2 3 + 4

59.

V∧V∧V∧V∧
1 + 2 + 3 + 4 +

60.

V∧V∧V∧V∧
1 + 2 + 3 + 4 +

61.

V∧V∧V∧V∧
1 + 2 + 3 + 4 +

62.

V∧V∧V∧V∧
1 + 2 + 3 + 4 +

63.

V∧V∧V∧V∧
1 + 2 + 3 + 4 +

64. Jamaica Farewell

Rhythm Pattern
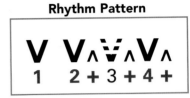

Down the way   where the nights are gay __   and the sun shines dai-ly on the

moun-tain-top,   I took a trip   on a   sai - ling ship   and when I

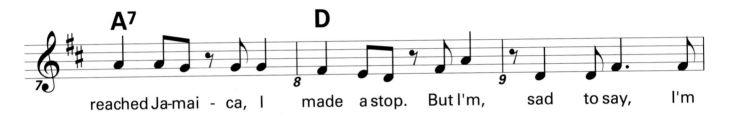

reached Ja-mai - ca, I   made a stop. But I'm,   sad   to say,   I'm

on   my way,   won't   be back   for ma-ny a day, __   my

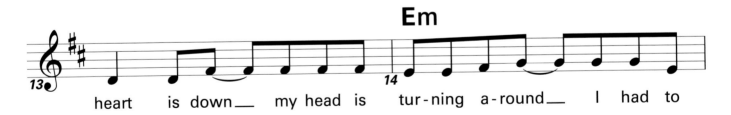

heart   is down __ my head is   tur -ning a -round __   I had to

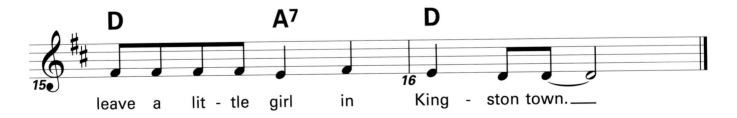

leave   a   lit - tle   girl   in   King - ston town. __

65. Waltzing Matilda

This is Australia's most famous folk song. It contains almost all of the chords you have learned up to this point. Take it slowly until you can comfortably play it without mistakes. Then gradually increase the tempo.

Rhythm Pattern

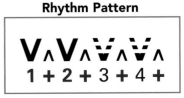

Once a jol-ly swag-man camped by a bill-a-bong un - der the shade of a

coo-li-bar tree and he sang as he watched and wait-ed till his bil-ly boiled,

you'll come a waltz - ing Ma - til - da with me. Waltz - ing Ma - til - da,

Waltz - ing Ma-til - da, you'll come a waltz - ing Ma - til - da with me, and his

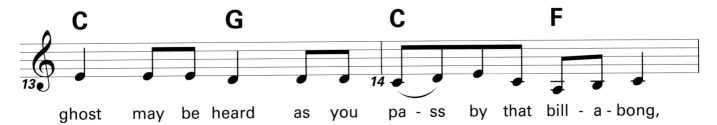

ghost may be heard as you pa - ss by that bill - a - bong,

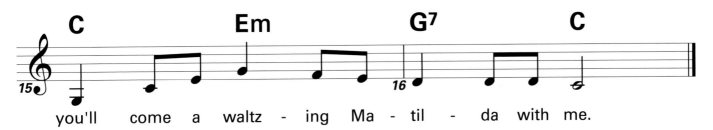

you'll come a waltz - ing Ma - til - da with me.

C7

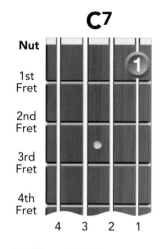

Nut
1st Fret
2nd Fret
3rd Fret
4th Fret

4 3 2 1

C Seventh Chord

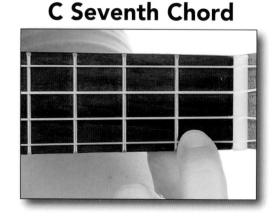

Chord Symbol

To play the **C7** chord, use the **first** finger of your left hand as shown in the diagram, and strum all **four** strings.

 66.

Practice changing from **Am** to **C7** and **C7** to **F**, then play the whole progression and finish with an **F** chord.

Rhythm Pattern

V∧V∧V V
1 + 2 + 3 4

| F | Dm | Am | C7 |

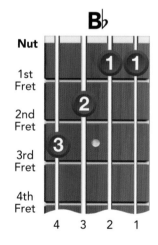

B♭

Nut
1st Fret
2nd Fret
3rd Fret
4th Fret

4 3 2 1

B Flat Major Chord

Chord Symbol

To play the **B♭** chord, use the **first, second** and **third** fingers of your left hand as shown in the diagram. Strum **all four** strings.

 67.

Make sure you are comfortable changing to and from **B♭** before playing this progression.

Rhythm Pattern

V∧V∧V V
1 + 2 + 3 4

| F | B♭ | C7 | F |

The following song is in the key of F and uses the chords **F**, **B♭** and **C7**. Make sure you are comfortable with all the chord changes and then try them with the strumming pattern. Once you can play the song slowly, gradually increase the tempo until you can play it along with the recording.

 68. Under the Bamboo Tree

B⁷

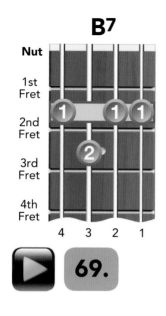

Nut
1st Fret
2nd Fret
3rd Fret
4th Fret

4 3 2 1

B Seventh Chord

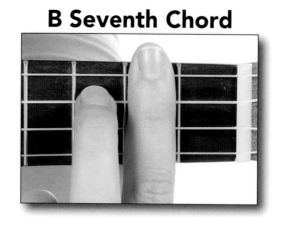

Chord Symbol

To play the **B7** chord, use the **first** and **second** fingers of your left hand as shown in the diagram. Strum **all four** strings.

Rhythm Pattern

V V∧⩔∧V
1 2 + 3 + 4

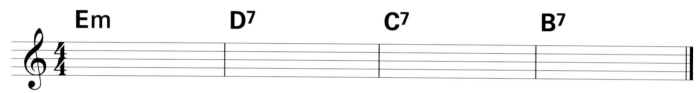

Em   D⁷   C⁷   B⁷

E

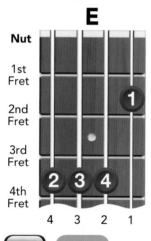

Nut
1st Fret
2nd Fret
3rd Fret
4th Fret

4 3 2 1

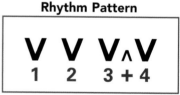

E Major Chord

Chord Symbol

E

To play the **E** chord, use **all four** fingers of your left hand as shown in the diagram. Strum all **four** strings.

Rhythm Pattern

V V V∧V
1 2 3 + 4

Practice all the chord changes separately and then play the whole progression. Notice that there are two chords in bar 7.

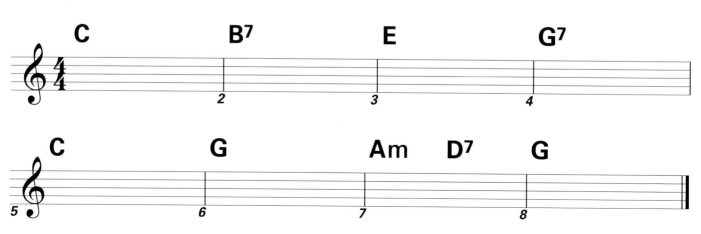

C   B⁷   E   G⁷
2   3   4

C   G   Am   D⁷   G
5   6   7   8

The timing of basic note values, rhythms and rests are illustrated in the following table.

NOTES, RHYTHMS AND RESTS

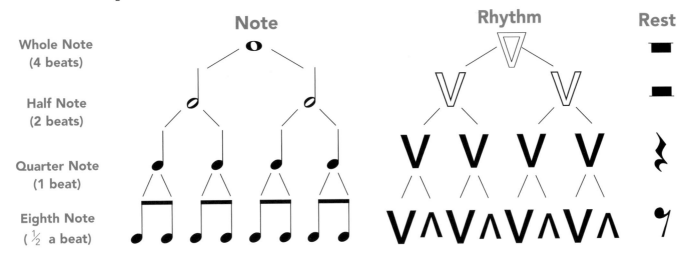

	Note	Rhythm	Rest
Whole Note (4 beats)			
Half Note (2 beats)			
Quarter Note (1 beat)			
Eighth Note (½ a beat)			

RHYTHM NOTATION

As well as traditional music notation and tablature, Ukulele music sometimes uses **rhythm notation**. This is similar to traditional notation, except that the notes have a diagonal line instead of a notehead. This tells you that instead of playing individual notes, you will be strumming chords. The names of the chords to be played are written above the notation, as shown in the example on the following page.

 71.

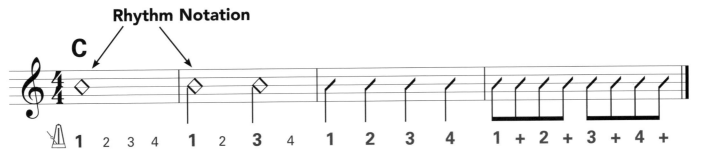

Notice the ties in the rhythm notation shown below. The tie tells you to hold the chord until the next chord is due to be strummed. This may look complex but it is simply a notated version of the rhythm pattern shown above the notation.

Rhythm Pattern

V V∧⩒∧V
1 2 + 3 + 4

72.

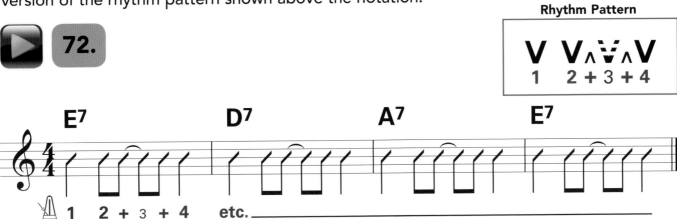

RESTS

A rest is used to indicate a specific period of silence. The following diagrams show three different rest values. The **quarter rest** is worth **one beat** of silence, the **half rest** worth **two beats** of silence and the **whole rest** worth **one whole bar** of silence. Small counting numbers are placed under rests. Note that the half rest sits on top of the middle line of the staff, while the whole rest hangs below the fourth line.

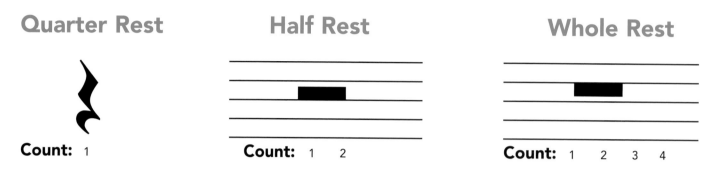

Quarter Rest	Half Rest	Whole Rest
Count: 1	**Count:** 1 2	**Count:** 1 2 3 4

When a rest occurs after you have played a note, you must stop the note sounding, i.e., stop the strings vibrating. This can be done by placing your left hand fingers lightly across all the strings. Do not press too hard as this will produce a new note. This **muting** technique is also useful to stop previously played notes sounding at the same time as a new note is played.

When chords are played, rests are achieved by stopping all four strings sounding by placing the edge of the right hand over the strings (as shown in the photograph).

 **73.**

This example demonstrates the use of quarter rests along with quarter notes.

STACCATO

A dot above or below a note or chord indicates that the note or chord is to be played **staccato**, which means short and separate from other notes or chords.

PLAYING CHORDS STACCATO

It is not always desirable to leave a chord ringing once it has been played. Playing some of the chords staccato can make the rhythm sound much tighter and give a feeling of movement and life to a chord progression. With chords containing open strings, staccato is usually achieved by placing the side of the right hand across all the strings immediately after strumming the chord. Practice this on one chord until you have control of the technique and then try the following example.

74. Blues in E

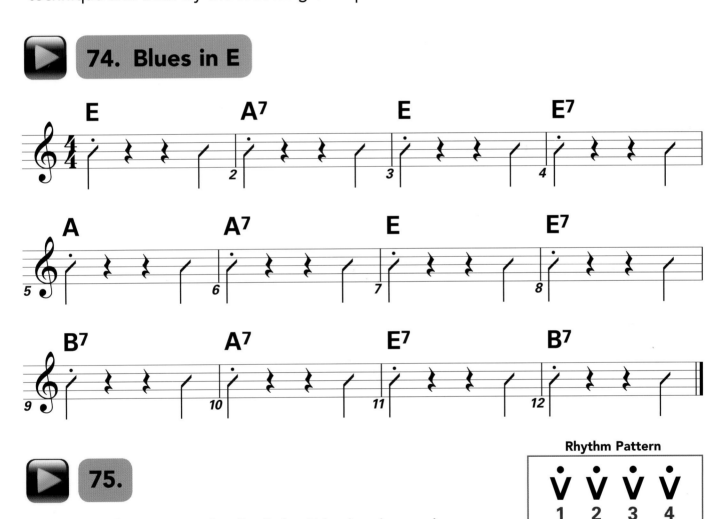

75.

Rhythm Pattern

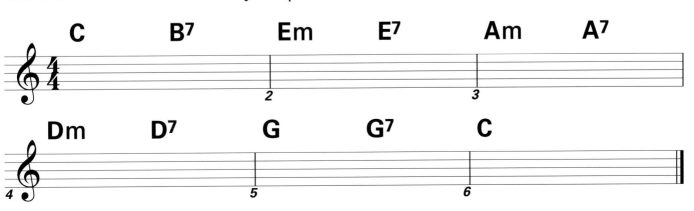

This example uses nearly all of the 7th chords you have learned. Notice the staccato rhythm pattern.

LESSON FOURTEEN

DIMINISHED CHORDS

The chord symbol for a **diminished** chord is ^o or **dim**. The full name of this chord is diminished seventh but it is usually referred to as a diminished chord. Here is the most common chord shape for the diminished chord.

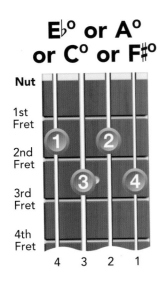

**E♭° or A°
or C° or F♯°**

Chord Symbol

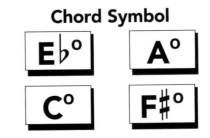

This diminished chord shape has **four different names**. The diminished chord can take its name from **any note** in the chord, e.g., the shape to the left contains the notes **E flat (E♭)**, **C**, **A** and **F sharp (F♯)**. So this shape can be either **E♭dim**, **Cdim**, **Adim** or **F♯dim.** If this shape was moved up one fret it would be **Edim** or **C♯dim**, **B♭dim** or **Gdim** etc. To locate any diminished chord simply play this diminished shape so that it includes the letter name of the chord.

▶ 76.

▶ 77.

AUGMENTED CHORDS

The chord symbol for an augmented chord is **+** or **aug**. Here is the most common chord shape for the augmented chord.

D⁺ or F♯⁺ or B♭⁺

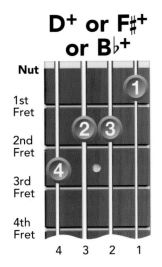

Chord Symbol

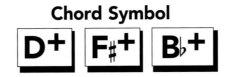

The augmented chord can take its name from **any note** in the chord, e.g., the shape shown here contains the notes **D**, **F♯** and **B♭** (twice). This chord can either be **Daug**, **F♯aug**, or **B♭aug**. This shape is movable so it can be played in any position. If this shape was moved up one fret, it would be **E♭aug**, **Gaug** or **Baug** etc. To locate any augmented chord, simply play the movable version of the augmented shape so that it includes the letter name of the chord.

C⁺ or E⁺ or A♭⁺

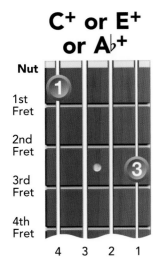

Chord Symbol

If the previous chord was moved two frets higher to achieve **Caug**, **Eaug** or **Aaug**, it would be hard to play and sound thin. The chord shown here sounds much better and is easier to play.

78.

Rhythm Pattern

V V∧V∧V
1 2 + 3 + 4

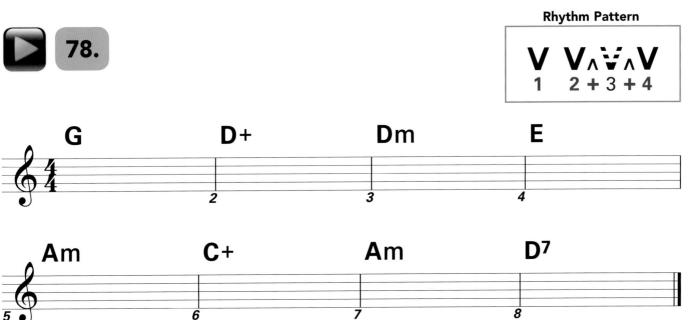

LESSON FIFTEEN

EIGHTH NOTE TRIPLET RHYTHMS

Count: 1   +   a
Say: one   and   ah

Eighth note triplet rhythms are **three** evenly spaced strums within one beat. One bar of eighth note triplets in $\frac{4}{4}$ time would consist of **four** groups of **three** strums. There are **12 strums** per bar but still only **four beats**. Notice that there are two downstrums in this pattern; **down up down**. This means you will play two downstrums in a row between the third part of one beat and the first part of the next beat. Play the first downstrum of each group of three louder.

 79.

Practice this rhythm pattern holding a **C** chord.

Triplet Rhythm Pattern

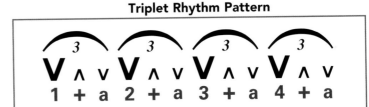

 80.

Play the following chord progression using the above triplet rhythm pattern.

C   Am   F   G⁷

 81.

This example uses a triplet rhythm on the **second** and **third** beats.

Triplet Rhythm Pattern

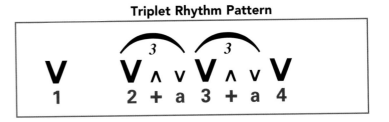

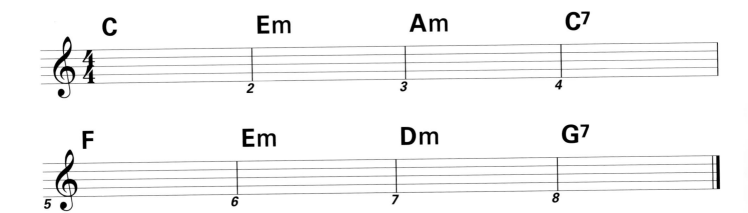

C   Em   Am   C⁷

F   Em   Dm   G⁷

82. Triplet City

Triplet Rhythm Pattern

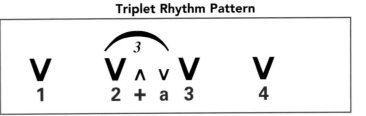

Here is a 12 bar Jazz Blues progression using a triplet on the second beat. Notice the use of augmented and diminished chords in this progression. These chords are commonly used in Jazz.

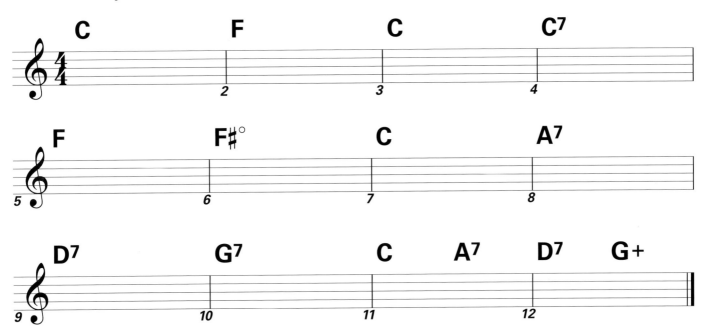

 83. St James Infirmary

This traditional song was made famous by **Louis Armstrong** and has been played by many of the great Jazz players.

Triplet Rhythm Pattern

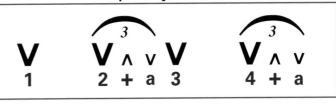

LESSON SIXTEEN

SWING RHYTHMS

Many songs are played using a swing rhythm because it creates a great momentum. It first became popular as a dance rhythm in Jazz, Blues, Gospel and Pop music in the early 20th century. A **swing rhythm** can be created by tying the first two notes of the triplet group together.

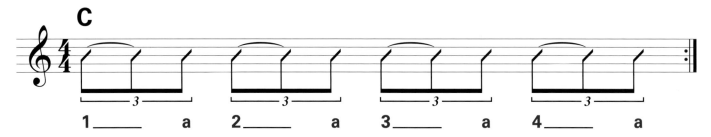

The two eighth note triplets tied together in the example above can be replaced by a quarter note.

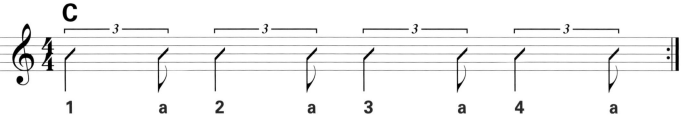

To simplify notation, it is common to replace the ♪ ♪ with ♪ ♪ , and to write at the start of the piece ♫ = ♩ ♪ as illustrated below.

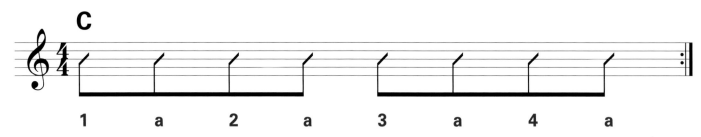

Swing rhythms can also be applied to rhythm patterns. In the following pattern, the eighth notes in the second and fourth beats are swung. Listen to the recording and then play the rhythm holding a **C chord**.

87.

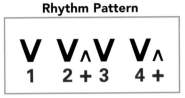

Rhythm Pattern

V	V	∧	V	V	∧
1	2	+	3	4	+

Now apply the swung rhythm pattern to the following song.

88. Aloha Oe

Rhythm Pattern

V	V	∧	V	V	∧
1	2	+	3	4	+

Fare - well   my   love,   fare - well   to

thee,   while   you're a - way   I'll   pray for your re - turn -

ing,   One   fond   em - brace,   one   kiss   and

then,   fare - well   un - til   we meet a - gain._____

MAJOR SEVENTH CHORDS

Another chord type you will need to know is the **major seventh**. The major seventh chord symbol is **maj7**. Here are some common open chord shapes for **maj7** chords.

Cmaj7

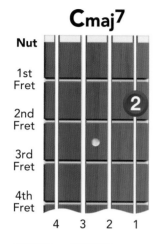

C Major Seventh Chord

Chord Symbol

Cmaj7

To play the **Cmaj7** chord, use the **second** finger of your left hand as shown in the diagram. Strum **all four** strings.

 89.

Rhythm Pattern

V V∧V∧V∧
1 2 + 3 + 4 +

Cmaj7   Am   F   G7

Fmaj7

F Major Seventh Chord

Chord Symbol

Fmaj7

To play the **Fmaj7** chord, use **all four** fingers of your left hand as shown in the diagram. Strum **all four** strings.

 90.

Rhythm Pattern

V V̇ V V̇
1 2 3 4

Cmaj7 Fmaj7   Cmaj7 Fmaj7   Cmaj7 Fmaj7   Dm   G7

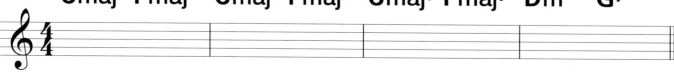

Gmaj⁷

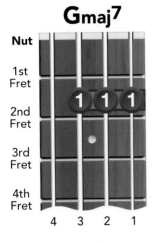

G Major Seventh Chord

To play the **Gmaj7** chord, use the **first** finger of your left hand as shown in the diagram. Strum **all four** strings.

 **91.**

Triplet Rhythm Pattern

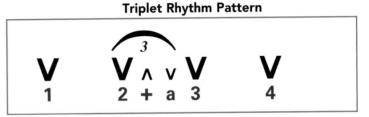

Gmaj⁷   Cmaj⁷   Fmaj⁷   Dm   Cmaj⁷

Amaj⁷

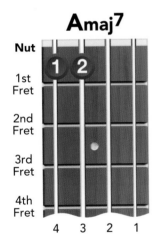

A Major Seventh Chord

Chord Symbol

Amaj⁷

To play the **Amaj7** chord, use the **first** and **second** fingers of your left hand as shown in the diagram. Strum **all four** strings.

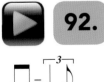 **92.**

Rhythm Pattern

A   Amaj⁷   D   E⁷

MINOR SEVENTH CHORDS

Another chord type you will need to know is the **minor seventh**. The minor seventh chord symbol is **m7**. Here are the most common open chord shapes for **m7** chords.

Dm⁷

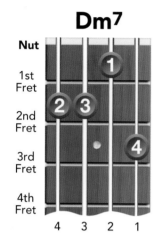

Nut
1st Fret
2nd Fret
3rd Fret
4th Fret

4 3 2 1

D Minor Seventh Chord

Chord Symbol

Dm⁷

To play the **Dm7** chord, use **all four** fingers of your left hand as shown in the diagram. Strum **all four** strings.

 93.

Rhythm Pattern

V V∧V∧V∧
1 2 + 3 + 4 +

Cmaj⁷   **Am**   **Dm⁷**   **G⁷**

Am⁷

Nut
1st Fret
2nd Fret
3rd Fret
4th Fret

4 3 2 1

A Minor Seventh Chord

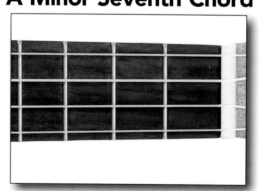

Chord Symbol

Am⁷

To play the **Am7** chord, strum **all four** open strings. **No fingers** are required for this chord.

 94.

Rhythm Pattern

V V̇ V V̇
1 2 3 4

Dm⁷ G⁷   **Cmaj⁷ Fmaj⁷ Dm⁷ E⁷**   **Am⁷ A⁷**

Em⁷ — E Minor Seventh Chord

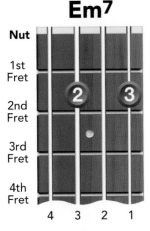

Chord Symbol

Em⁷

To play the **Em7** chord, use the **second** and **third** fingers of your left hand as shown in the diagram. Strum **all four** strings.

 95.

An **Em7** chord is used in this exercise.

Rhythm Pattern

V ∧ V ∧ V ∧ V
1 + 2 + 3 + 4

| Gmaj⁷ | Em⁷ | Am⁷ | D⁷ |

 96. Minor Detour

Here is a Blues progression using minor 7th chords. Notice also the use of **Fmaj7** and **E7**. In many Blues and Jazz songs, most of the chords are sevenths.

Rhythm Pattern

V V ∧ V ∧ V
1 2 + 3 + 4

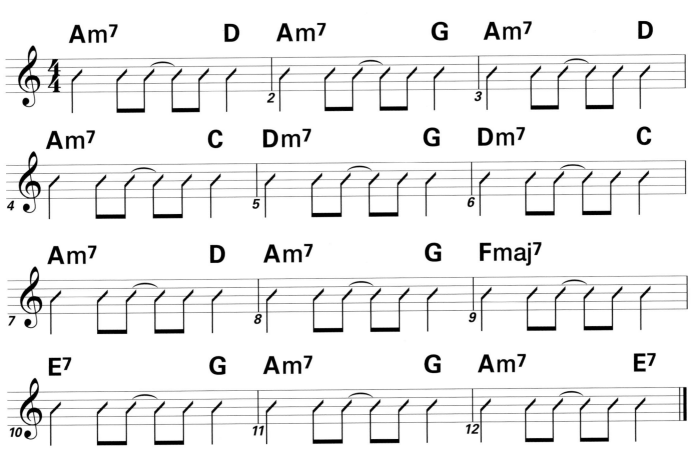

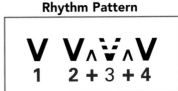

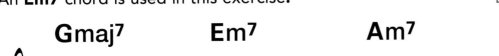

LESSON NINETEEN

COMPING

Comping is the Jazz term for accompaniment, which includes the art of complementing the soloist with what you play. To do this you need a good knowledge of chords and how to use them, and you must be familiar with Jazz rhythms and approaches to rhythm playing on the Ukulele.

You also need to be a sensitive listener, with the ability to respond quickly to other musicians. This is best developed through a great deal of listening and improvising.

FOUR TO THE BAR

A good way to consolidate your knowledge of note and rest values is to practice them as a set rhythm when playing through a chord progression. This traditional Jazz rhythm pattern is known as "four to the bar", which simply means four quarter note strums per bar. It is a good rhythm to play when learning a new set of chord changes.

Rhythm Pattern

V	V	V	V
1	2	3	4

97. Shine on Harvest Moon

Shine on, shine on har - vest moon, ____ up in the sky, I ain't had no lo - vin' since Jan-u - a - ry, Feb-ru - a - ry, June or Ju - ly.__ Snow time ain't no time to stay,____ out doors and spoon, so shine on, shine on har-vest moon for me and my gal.

THE CHARLESTON RHYTHM

Instead of playing the standard four to the bar rhythm, it often sounds effective to play the Ukulele like a horn section, using short punchy rhythms and whole or partial chords. Many rhythms used by horn sections can be transferred directly to the Ukulele. One of the most common is known as the Charleston rhythm (named after the dance, but originally from Africa). Here is the basic rhythm applied to a turnaround progression.

98.

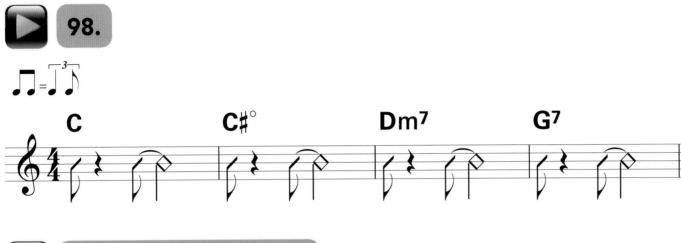

99. Charleston Crazy

The following chord progression is similar to the song "The Charleston" and also "Has Anybody Seen My Gal?". The Charleston rhythm works well with many popular songs from the early 20th century.

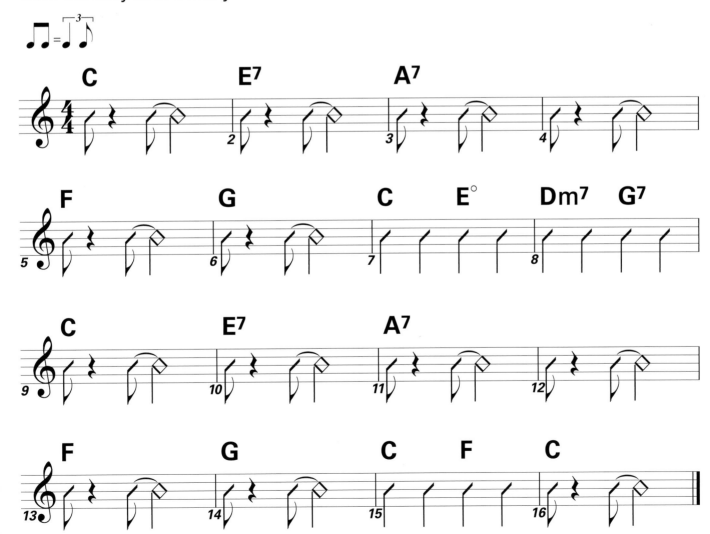

By varying the length of the notes and moving the Charleston rhythm one eighth note at a time, it is possible to create many variations which are useful for comping. Learn the rhythms shown below on one chord and then try applying them to a set of chord changes.

100.

Am⁷

RHYTHM CHANGES

The term **Rhythm Changes** refers to a progression based on the George Gershwin song **I Got Rhythm**. Over the years there have been many new melodies (or **heads** in Jazz terms) written on this progression and it is still routinely used by musicians jamming together or auditioning a new band member.

The example on the following page shows the basic progression in the key of **B flat**. Try comping along with the recording, using your knowledge of chords and keys, but also relying on your ear. This recording is quite fast, so if you have trouble with it, practice the progression with a metronome first. Start out slowly and then increase the tempo once you can play it perfectly.

There are several new chords used in this song. The chord fingerings are shown below.

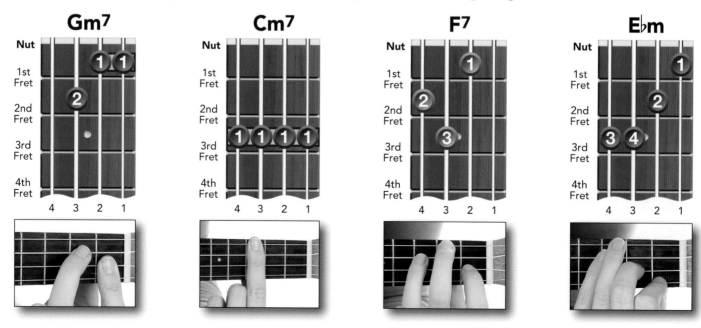

Gm⁷	Cm⁷	F7	E♭m

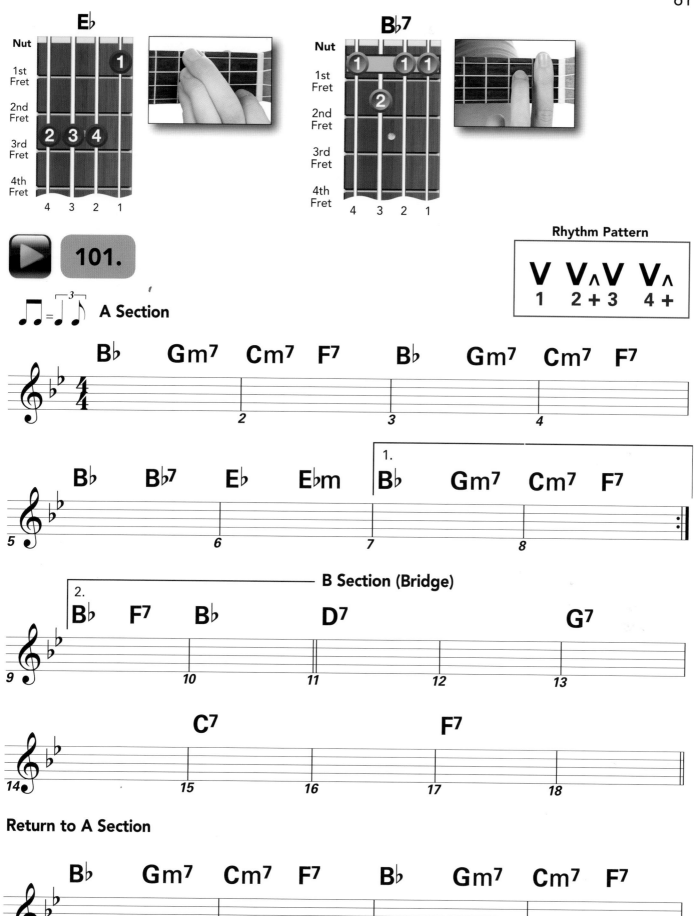

LESSON TWENTY

NINTH CHORDS

Another chord type you will need to know to play Swing, Jazz, Blues or Ragtime is the ninth chord. Shown below are the fingerings for A9, D9 and E9.

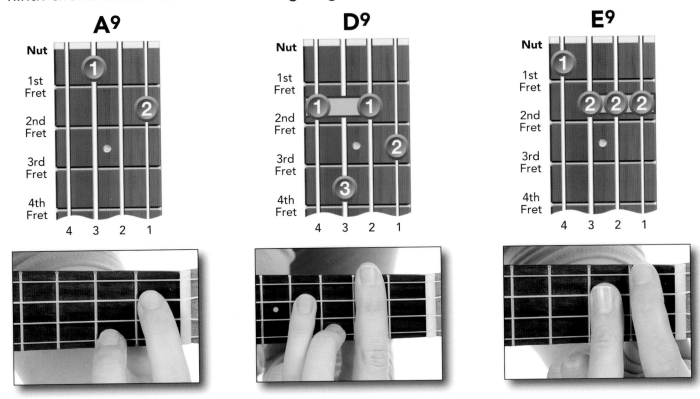

Now try the following Blues which uses all three of these ninth chords.

102. Ninety Nine Blues

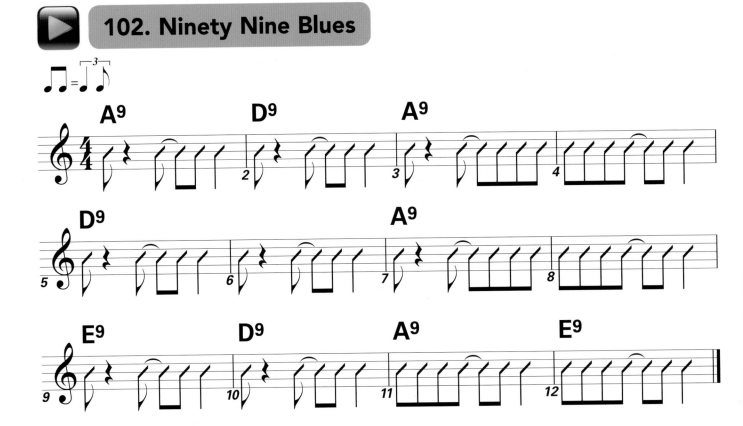

63

103. For Me and My Gal

HOW TO READ SHEET MUSIC

Most of the sheet music you will buy will be arranged for piano. Piano music is written using two or three staves, with the chord symbols written above the top staff. It may also contain unfamiliar symbols and terms. At this stage you need only look at the top staff, which contains the melody line (tune), the lyrics and the chords. In some sheet music, chord diagrams may also be included. As most sheet music is arranged by keyboard players there are often no Ukulele chord shapes, or there may be guitar chord shapes.

Also many piano arrangements are in difficult keys for a beginning Ukulele player and quite often use unnecessary chords. Piano sheet music also gives no indication of how to strum the chords. So piano sheet music is only a guide for a uke player but is useful for lyrics and a general chord guide.

If the song contains chords that you are not familiar with you can:

1. **Learn how to play this new chord.**
    Refer to the chord chart on the following pages.

2. **Substitute an easier chord.**
    Use the easy chord table below which lists the type of chord you may see in the sheet music (on the left of the table) and the simpler chord you can substitute (on the right of the table). If you know how to transpose and substitute chords you can play almost every song ever written using only a few basic chord shapes.

EASY CHORD TABLE

When you see an unfamiliar chord, consult the table below to find an easier chord to play. This chord will still sound correct. For example, when you see a **Cmaj7** symbol, play a **C** chord instead. For a **Cm6**, you can substitute a **Cm** chord, etc.

Chord Written on Sheet Music			Use This Chord
7	-	Seventh	**Major**
6	-	Sixth	
maj7	-	Major Seventh	
sus	-	Suspended	
9	-	9th	**Seventh (7)**
11	-	Eleventh	
13	-	Thirteenth	
m6	-	Minor Sixth	**Minor (m)**
m7	-	Minor Seventh	
m(maj)7	-	Minor Major Seventh	

3. **Change the key of the song.**
    Transposing (or **Transposition**) is the process of changing a song or piece of music from one key to another.

    There are two reasons for transposing into another key:
    A. If the song is too high or too low to sing, the song can be changed into a lower or higher key. Changing the key of a song does not change the sound, pattern or timing of the melody but simply changes how high or how low it is sung.

    B. If the song is hard to play or contains difficult chords you can transpose it to a key with easier chords. For example, if a song is written in the key of **B♭** (which many songs are) it would contain chords like **B♭**, **E♭** and **Cm** which may be difficult for a beginner. If the song is transposed into the key of G major the chords would then be **G**, **C** and **Am**, which are easier to play on the Ukulele.

HOW TO TRANSPOSE

If the sheet music is in the key of **E flat (E♭) major** and contains difficult chord shapes, you can transpose it to another major key with easier chord shapes. Keys that contain easy shapes for beginners are **C major** and **G major**, or if the song is in a minor key, **A minor (Am)** or **E minor (Em)**.

Write down the chromatic scale (see below) of the key the sheet music is in (usually the first chord is the key chord). Then underneath it write down the chromatic scale of the key you wish to change to. For example, to change a song from the key of **E♭** to the key of **G**, write down the chromatic scale starting with the note **E♭** and then underneath it write down the chromatic scale starting on the note **G**.

E♭ chromatic scale:	E♭	E	F	G♭	G	A♭	A	B♭	B	C	D♭	D	E♭
	↓	↓	↓	↓	↓	↓	↓	↓	↓	↓	↓	↓	↓
G chromatic scale:	G	G♯	A	A♯	B	C	C♯	D	D♯	E	F	F♯	G

The letter name of the chord is written on the top line and the letter name of the new chord in the new key (in this case **G**) will be directly underneath it.

Note that the chord type never changes. If the chord is a minor chord in the key of **E♭ major** it will also be a minor chord in the major key it is transposed to.

E.g., an **E♭** chord in the key of **E♭ major** becomes a **G** chord in the key of **G major**.
E.g., an **A♭** chord in the key of **E♭ major** becomes a **C** chord in the key of **G major**.
E.g., a **Cm** chord in the key of **E♭ major** becomes an **Em** chord in the key of **G major**.
E.g., a **B♭m** chord in the key of **E♭ major** becomes a **Dm** chord in the key of **G major**.

The easiest keys for Ukulele are:
G major, C major, D major, A major, E major, A minor and **E minor**. These keys contain chords that have open strings in them, which are generally easier to hold.

CHORD CHART

Here is a chart of the types of chords you will most commonly find in sheet music. The shapes given are all based around the first few frets. These open chords sound particularly good on the Ukulele.

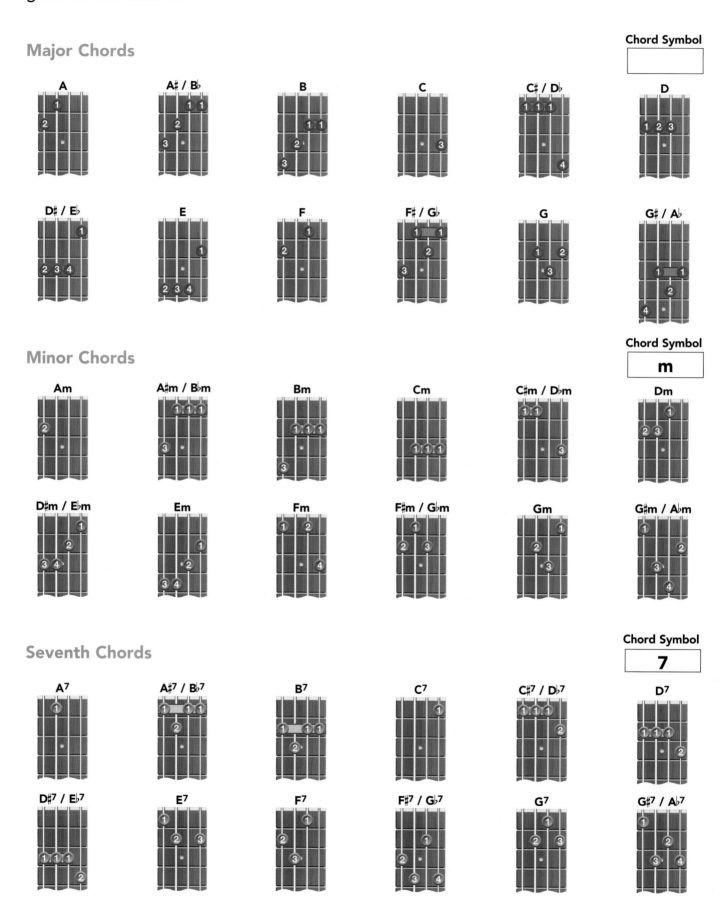

Minor Seventh Chords

Chord Symbol **m⁷**

Am⁷ 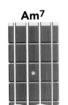 Bm⁷  Cm⁷  Dm⁷  Em⁷  Fm⁷  Gm⁷

Major Seventh Chords

Chord Symbol **maj⁷**

Amaj⁷  Bmaj⁷ Cmaj⁷ Dmaj⁷  Emaj⁷ Fmaj⁷ Gmaj⁷

Major Sixth Chords

Chord Symbol **6**

A⁶  B⁶  C⁶ D⁶  E⁶ F⁶ G⁶

Suspended Chords

Chord Symbol **sus**

Asus  Bsus 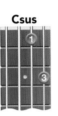 Csus  Dsus Esus  Fsus  Gsus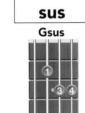

Ninth Chords

Chord Symbol **9**

A⁹  B⁹  C⁹ D⁹  E⁹  F⁹ G⁹

Augmented Chords

Chord Symbol **aug or +**

A⁺ 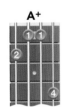 B⁺  C⁺ D⁺  E⁺  F⁺  G⁺

Diminished Chords

Chord Symbol **dim or °**

A°  B°  C°  D°  E°  F°  G°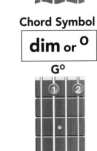

www.learntoplaymusic.com

TUNING YOUR UKULELE TO THE RECORDING

On the accompanying DVDs and DVD-ROM, the four open strings of the Ukulele are played. You should tune each string of your Ukulele to each of these notes. These notes are the same pitch as an electronic tuner so if you have tuned using an electronic tuner your Ukulele will be in tune with the recording.

The first note played is the open **4th** string (a **G** note).

If the open **4th** string on your Ukulele sounds the same as the note on the recording, your string is **in tune**. Proceed to the next string.

If the note on the recording sounds **higher**, it means your **4th** string (a **G** note) is **flat**. Turn the tuning key slowly in a counter-clockwise direction. This will raise the pitch of your string. Play your **4th** string again and compare it with the recording. Keep doing this until your **4th** string sounds the same as the recording. Usually you will not have to turn the tuning key very far.

If the note on the recording sounds **lower**, it means your **4th** string is **sharp**. Turn the tuning key slowly in a clockwise direction. This will lower the pitch of your string. Play your **4th** string again and compare it with the recording. Keep doing this until your **4th** string is the same as the recording.

Follow this procedure for the other strings.

To check if your Ukulele is in tune strum a **chord** (see Lesson One). Most students find it easier to tune up to a note, so you may wish to detune your string to slightly below the recording, and tune up from there.

TUNING TO ANOTHER INSTRUMENT

If you are playing along with another instrument, it is essential that your Ukulele be in tune with that instrument. Tune the open strings of your Ukulele to the corresponding notes of the accompanying instrument. E.g., to tune to a piano, tune the open 4th string to the **G** note on the

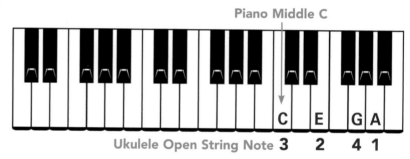

piano, as shown on the keyboard diagram. Then tune your Ukulele to itself from this note using the method outlined next, or tune each string of your Ukulele to those notes of the piano shown on the keyboard diagram.

TUNING THE UKULELE TO ITSELF

Unless you are using an electronic tuner, to be able to tune the Ukulele accurately usually requires many months of practice. You will probably need your music teacher or musician friend to help you tune when you are learning.

If you do not have another instrument to tune to, you can tune the Ukulele to itself by using the following method.

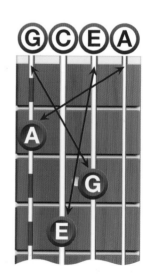

1. Tune the open **4th** string (a **G** note) to the recording, pitch pipe or to another instrument. If these options are not available then tune the string to a familiar pitch and assume the string is in tune.
2. Tune the **open 1st string** (an **A** note) to the same pitch as the **second** fret of the **4th** string.
3. Tune the **2nd** string until the note on the **third** fret of the **2nd** string (a **G** note) is the same pitch as the open **4th** string.
4. Tune the **3rd** string until the note on the **fourth** fret of the **3rd** string (an **E** note) is the same pitch as the open **2nd** string.